Poems of Everyday Life

Suzanne W. Guinn

WestBow
PRESS®
A DIVISION OF THOMAS NELSON
& ZONDERVAN

WestBow Press books may be ordered through booksellers or by contacting:

WestBow Press
A Division of Thomas Nelson & Zondervan
1663 Liberty Drive
Bloomington, IN 47403
www.westbowpress.com
844-714-3454

ISBN: 978-1-6642-4888-5 (sc)
ISBN: 978-1-6642-4887-8 (e)

Print information available on the last page.

WestBow Press rev. date: 12/10/2021

Biography

Suzanne Guinn began writing poetry at the encouragement of her high school English teacher, Mrs. Agnus Smith. She has expressed herself through many styles of poetry and on a variety of subjects. She loves the creativity that poetry brings. Having a musical background in her education, (BS, 1972), the writing of poetry is a natural step in using words with their rhythmic ways. She also expresses her creativity in fine art paintings, jewelry design, photography and more. She is a wife, mother of 4 and grand-mother of 6. Though a native of New York State she has lived in the Midwest or South since the age of 8. She earned her graduate degree in Library Science and later retired in 2014 after 30 years in her field. She currently is retired and resides in Kansas.

Suzanne W. Guinn

Dewey number: 811
LC number: PS 301

Dedication

This little book is dedicated to my friend and fellow poet, Bruce Bergstrom who inspires me with his accomplishments and his good humor. And to my High School Teacher, Mrs. Agnus Smith who started me on this journey, with lots of encouragement, advice and friendship.

Introduction
And
Prologue

This is a collection of random poems written over several years, beginning in High School and a first attempt at publishing. In recent years I've had several ask if I have published my work or have I ever thought of doing this. So this is the result of that encouragement. About half of the poetry I write comes from my walk with the Lord. Inspiration comes from a variety of ways. Sometimes it is a phrase or comment someone has said. Sometimes, it is a thought that pops into my head.

Artwork and photography are also by yours truly. It is my hope that you will enjoy, and be blessed and encouraged by the readings.

Thanks go to Jay Hale, who proofread, edited and advised in the adventure.

Table of Contents

Illustrations:

Front Cover—Kitchen Still Life, (water color)
Back Cover—Angels Sent Calling, and Jesus-Light of the World, (both colored pencil)
Facebook page: "Suzanne Wagner Guinn"
Email: wagnersisters @yahoo.com
website: wagnersisters.weebly.com

Poems of Everyday Life

It's Jesus

It's Jesus who lay in yonder stall.
It's Jesus of whom the angels sing.
It's Jesus on whom the shepherds call.
It's Jesus who was visited by kings.

It's Jesus in the carpenter's shop.
It's Jesus sitting in the temple teaching.
It's Jesus tempted on mountain top.
It's Jesus in the pastures, preaching.

It's Jesus raising the sick from the bed.
It's Jesus feeding the growing throngs.
It's Jesus raising his friend from the dead.
It's Jesus who brings right from wrongs.

It's Jesus who came to die for all.
It's Jesus who came, our debt to pay.
It's Jesus on whom we all must call.
It's Jesus of whom we rejoice this day.

2019

I'm Tired

I'm tired says the little boy coming in from play.
He takes a short nap and soon is on his way.
It doesn't take long to get his strength renewed.

I'm tired says the teenager who is growing like the weeds.
He sleeps long hours, getting rest for that is what he needs.
College life is coming when late nights are pursued.

I'm tired says the mother exhausted from her life.
Her nights are short and days are filled with strife.
Yet with her second wind she goes about her day.

I'm tired says the grandpa whose life has caught up with him.
His strength has waned and his eyes are growing dim.
His weary bones now rattle, he's walked a long, hard way.

I'm tired says the saint who longs for heavenly rest.
"I've served my Lord my whole life, I hope I've done my best."
"Come home, oh weary soul, through Heaven's open door."

You've played and worked, and strove through life,
With the goal to live with the Lord in the afterlife.
"Come rest in pastures lush and green, come rest forever more."

2019

Angels

Angels came from heaven to earth,
Announced to us His holy birth.
They told the shepherds where to go,
Their faces bright with heavenly glow.

They watch o'er us throughout the night.
They care for us with all their might.
Their mighty power is oft revealed.
Their gentle touch is not concealed.

They're white as snow on a winter's day.
They're soft like breeze o'er new mown hay.
They're quick and strong like rushing streams.
Their light is bright like morning beams.

Although here they have a special place,
They work beyond earth's time and space.
Their jobs are many, not a few,
Including taking care of me and you.

1994

Beauty

Beauty is found anywhere.
On the leaf, in the pear.
No need to look very far.
You can find it where you are.

1966

Because He Died and Rose Again

Today the evil of man's heart
Fills the world in very part.
The devil's plan from the start?
To keep the Lord and man apart.

But being God, He had a plan
To bring redemption to sinful man.
His Son became a child of man
And took God's news throughout the land.

So when your heart is filled with pain
Cause in the world evil men reign,
Recall God died and rose again,
And will return to ever reign.

His death, then life, brings hope we need
To cleanse our heart of hate and greed.
Then someday His plan will lead
To peace on earth, and from the curse - be freed.

2019

The Shell

That pretty shell
We all adore,
First had to die
Then come ashore.

1966

The Beach

While I walked down the beach everything within reach
Seemed to tug at my heart. From all of this I cannot part.
It was here I felt free and could live contentedly.
I am safe from the world, all it held, all it hurled.
This is my home meant for me, and the shell – my shade tree.
The sand of white is my grass, the waves my hills, oh alas!

1966

Long Out of School

Oh, where are the days of long ago
When off to school we would go?
There we learned to read and write.
We studied books from morn to night.

We worked our numbers, took some notes,
Studied tables, oft by rote.
Then one day our time had come.
Twelve years o'er, our days were done.

I'll always cherish those special days,
As friends have gone their separate ways.
The lessons learned, the golden rule,
Still guide my life, long out of school.

2016

Love, Divine

Jesus, you my lover be.
Hold me always close to thee.
Hold me in your loving arms.
Shield me, Lord, from worldly charms.
Shower me with love, divine.
Whisper softly, "Thou art mine."

Walk beside me, hold my hand,
Till we reach that Promised Land.
Keep your arm around my back.
Help me Lord to stay on track.
Shower me with love, divine.
Whisper softly, "Thou art mine.'"

When I hear your walking feet
My heart always skips a beat,
For I know we'll soon embrace.
My heart-filled sorrows you'll erase.
Shower me with love, divine.
Whisper softly, "Thou art mine."

As you stroke my silvered hair
And kiss away my tears of care,
Whisper softly in my ear
"I'll never leave you, do not fear."
Shower me with love, divine.
Whisper softly, "Thou art mine."

When you kiss me on my cheek,
Your perfumed face smells so sweet
I long for you, my lover, friend.
May this friendship never end.
Shower me with love, divine.
Whisper softly, "Thou art mine."

Hold me close next to your heart
So that I may ne'er depart.
But when e'er from you I stray,
Draw me back by end of day.
Shower me with love, divine.
Whisper softly, "Thou art mine."

On the cross you died for me.
You rose again on morning three.
Conquered death, my soul set free,
Thus your bride I'll always be.
Shower me with love, divine.
Whisper softly, "Thou art mine."

2019

Bless Me

Bless me, O Lord, I pray.
Bless me, O Lord, this day.
Cleanse my heart from sin.
Make me pure within.
Bless me, O Lord, I pray.

Bless me, O Lord, this day.
Bless me, O Lord, I pray.
Don't let me stray or part.
Guard and protect my heart.
Bless me, O Lord, I pray.

2011

The Real Christmas

Christmas isn't about Santa and his sleigh.
Christmas isn't even about the manger of hay.
Christmas isn't about the angels in the sky.
Christmas is about Jesus coming to die.

For Jesus brought the gifts that Christmas day.
He came to show us a much better way,
To give us redemption, salvation and life,
But not with the hoopla of Drummer and Fife.

He came as a baby one silent night,
To bring to dark souls his eternal light.
For only God could spread peace on earth,
And only because of our Savior's birth.

So, no matter the trappings by door or hearth,
It all comes down to what's in your heart.
Is it troubles and trials and unending strife,
Or God's gift of salvation and eternal life?

For whether we keep our traditions and ways,
Or keep it simple like all other days,
It's still Christmas for what God brings to us,
Not because of the hustle, hurry and fuss.

It's Christmas even when there's no tree in the house.
It's Christmas even if there's no socks, toys or blouse.
It's still Christmas when no stockings are being hung.
It's still Christmas. Hear the carols now being sung.

So, take time this Christmas to see the real truth,
The meaning of Christmas because of his birth,
Not the decorations, the wrappings or tree,
But because Jesus came to die, for you and me.

2019

Angels Sent Calling

"Archangel, Go to your post.
"Pass on the Word I gave you.
"Go ahead of the heavenly host,
"You have a special job to do."

He flew down through the universe
Passing stars and planets, bright,
Heading for the night side of earth,
Brightening the sky with heavenly light.

The angel found the roaming shepherds
Exactly where God said he would.
But frightened by the angel's sight,
The shepherds froze where each one stood.

He told the men the news of God -
A baby born, lays on the hay,
Who came to earth, His feet to trod,
To give His life, their debt to pay.

Then heavenly hosts soon gathered 'round
To join Ole Gabe and help him say
"All glory to the Most High God,
"For peace has come to man today."

When done the angels left the men,
Returning home from whence they came.
Though puzzled by the speech they sent,
They completed their task, just the same.

2018

The Cause

Two major wars fought on our soil,
Seemed deathly long, full of turmoil.
Homes were shattered, splitting the kin;
Each one thought right and sure to win.
With faith in God, His Word held true,
They all held a Christian view.

Soldiers fought then Sunday came.
Arms laid aside, they prayed the same.
Their faith in God brought foes together
Then back to the fight, their cause to further.

Now today you worship free,
Cause many died for liberty.
Yes, many died upon this land,
And shed their blood so you can stand
Or bow to pray on bended knees
Without fear that you will be seized.

Religious freedom in this land sublime
Was bought with blood so you could find
A place to live in our great land.
Just don't forget - "The Cause" - for which we stand.

2016

My Educated Raccoon

The bell has rung.
    They're on the run
        To their next class.

The lockers slam.
    The doors go 'bam!'
        Their eyes they cast

O'er the room.
    "Say, where's the coon
        You sneaked in here?"

The teacher screams,
    (Her face turns green),
        "Don't you come near!"

The girls did laugh.
    In marched the Staff;
        "What's all the noise?"

No girl would tell,
    Or could compel
        The naughty boys.

At Mr. Winkle
    The coon did wrinkle
        His cold black nose.

He did the 'Fish,'
    For Mr. Smith
        Then took a pose

Of Mr. Parks.
    While laughing hearts
        Filed out the room.

Here comes the bus.
    Don't make a fuss
        O'er my raccoon.

1967

The Gifts of Christmas

The gift of Christmas Love,
Sleeps on the hay, yet shines and glows.
The gift of Christmas Joy,
Warms our cold hearts and overflows.
The gift of Christmas Peace,
Calms fearful hearts and anxious souls.

The gift of Christmas Truth,
Reveals to man the living God.
The gift of Christmas Faith,
Gives guidance to the Christian's trod.
The gifts of the Christmas Child,
Bring hope to those who tread the sod.

2017

The Way in the Manger

Away in the manger, the cattle were lowing.
A baby lay wrapped while bright stars were glowing.
The shepherds were guarding when angels came calling,
Then leaving their sheep, they searched without stalling.

The message from angels in their hearts still burning,
They shared with neighbors, while to fields were returning.
Soon scholars came knocking, on what they were learning,
Leaving rulers and king, with troubled hearts churning.

For God became man, aft leaving His throne.
Our Father's promise from heaven had come -
Bringing to men salvation alone,
Providing for man the way to find Home.

2018

Trees

The trees send down roots, standing grand and tall,
Producing their leaves every spring,
Then shedding their leaves in the fall,
No matter what storms, of rain, snow or hail,
Or temperatures burning all day.

Lord, help me put down deep roots in the soil
Of Your precious Word for my heart,
Then harvest the fruit produced from my toil.
No matter the gifts, may I never fail,
Whatever my life brings my way.

2010

In the Beginning

"In the beginning God created,"
The first line in His Holy Word,
Speaks of God as a master artist,
Before telling us, He is our Lord.

First, He spoke and created Nature,
Displaying His glory and design,
Creating a place for His humans,
Planned before the beginning of time.

His creation is so infinite,
So vast and balanced, beyond wonder.
While detailed and so intricate,
It leaves us to marvel and ponder.

For the heavens reveal to the heathen
The story of a God with a plan.
The process was not without purpose -
That He would bring redemption to man.

His message is plain for all to see,

Revealed through His creativity,

His glory displayed to you and me,

And His love for all humanity.

2021

Angels Sent Calling

Colors of Fall

Blazing reds filter the morning sun.
Purple shades flitter when day is done.
Flaming oranges flicker as pumpkin lights.
Yellow golds glitter in moonlit nights.
Autumn hues glimmer in setting sun.
Winter snow's gleaming when autumn is done.

2011

Colors of Winter and Spring

Browns, blacks, blues, and grays -
These are the colors
Of winter's long days.

Pinks, reds, golds, and greens –
These are the colors
That new springtime preens.

Snow, wind, cold and ice -
These paint the pictures
That only look nice.

Warm days, breeze and showers -
These are the elements
That bring us the flowers.

Peace, joy, love, new life -
These things are all promised,
In God's Book of Life.

1995

This Dear Old Man

His quiet smile and strong warm hands
Gave strength and peace to life's demands.
His love for God and for His Word
Carved out his life and shaped his world.
Though loss was his from home to son,
He ne'er gave up. And everyone
That crossed his path knew it was true –
He loved the Lord and family, too.

He fixed our dolls and painted bikes.
When I was five he bought a kite,
Then hid it up above the door,
Till I spied it – now hid no more.
He worked all day till tasks were done
Then worked at home past set of sun.
He planted trees and tilled the ground;
His balding head and hands were brown.

No matter what the work at hand
From preaching Christ or clearing land
To fixing cars both old and new,
He gave his all, 'twas all he knew.
Though sweat was often on his brow
His kerchief band helped out somehow.
Then later when his knees were pained,
He never grumbled or complained.

His ethic of a workingman
Was written in his calloused hands,
So scarred and worn from years of toil.
Yet, 'twas my heart that gave him soil,
For there he planted seeds of truth
That he had taught me from my youth.
So then through life as he would stroll
He left his prints upon my soul.

Though born in means of low degree
And knew how hard that life could be
He used the gifts that God had given,
His heart and hands to help the livin'.
Now father's gone but left behind -
A heritage that now is mine.
I'll always miss this dear old man,
His loving heart and helping hands.

1994

Memories of Dad

Christmas Traditions

The calendar comes 'round for Christmas again,
With time set aside for families and friends,
For Christmas dinner and family filled seats,
Encircled by chatter and stories replete.

The table, all set with flowers and foods,
Pickles and giggles, 'n' home cooked goods.
Pies and cakes 'n' menus held dear
Are Christmas traditions renewed every year.

Grandma is waiting the families' return,
Hoping the next generation will learn,
That homecomings are always so special,
Treasured, and cherished, even essential.

2017

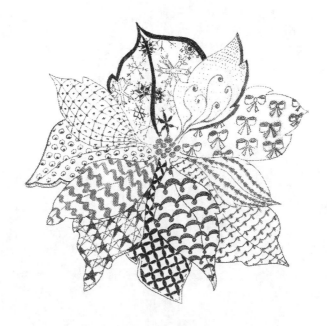

Happy New Year

Here's wishing you a Happy New Year,
Full of God's blessings every new day,
Times full of hope and heart filling peace,
Even if heartache troubles your way.

Times of success but not just in wealth,
Times of refreshing in your walk with the Lord,
Times of good days to bring you good health,
Times of renewal when reading God's word,

Days full of sunshine with just enough rain,
To fill up your pathway with blossoms of joy,
Filled with God's peace when inflicted by pain,
Knowing with Jesus you'll finish your voyage.

No matter the season, the day or the time,
Remember God's with you wherever you go.
For whether in sorrow or in good times,
Throughout the year, may God's glory show.

2018

My Mother's Voice

Down through the years
I always heard
My mother to me say:
Clean up your plate;
Please don't be late.
Did you brush your teeth today?
Put that back.
Don't touch that.
Please put your toys away.

Then as I grew the sayings changed
To fit the latest stage.
What is his name?
Where is the game?
And tell me what's his age?
Please call us dear.
How's school this year?
And also: how's your grades?

She also shared some other words
To teach me wrong from right,
To show me love
From God above
And give my pathway light.
Soft phrases meant
Encouragement
To live a life that's right.

Now time goes on and Mother's gone
Yet up here in my head,
I hear her say
Again today
The things she once had said.

Love God o'er all
Stand up tall
Put others first instead.

I now have children of my own
And to them I repeat
Those simple truths
Heard in my youth
That helped me guide my feet.
I hope that they
Will say someday
My Mom said this to me...

1993

Author's note:
My mother was a secretary
for many years. Thus, in her
memory, a typewriter type font
was used for this poem.

Jesus is My Nightlight

When troubles surround me and darkness fills my heart
I try to find my way and stumble in the dark
But when I turn to Jesus to help me ne'er depart
It's then I find He's been there from the start.

> Jesus is my nightlight in this darkened world of sin
> Showing me the footsteps through this world I'm in.
> Jesus is my night light as I journey on my way
> Lighting up the pathway like the light of day.

Now problems will attack us while in this world we roam
Filled with Satan's wicked and dirty little charms,
And trials will engulf us as we journey through this realm
For Satan wants to trip us, intent to cause us harm.

> Jesus is my nightlight in this darkened world of sin
> Showing me the footsteps through this world I'm in.
> Jesus is my night light as I journey on my way
> Lighting up the pathway like the light of day.

So, friend, if you're surrounded by the dark of night.
The answer to your troubles is let Jesus be your light.
He chases out the darkness from the path you trod.
He'll save you and will lead you to be at home with God.

> Jesus is my nightlight in this darkened world of sin
> Showing me the footsteps through this world I'm in.
> Jesus is my night light as I journey on my way
> Lighting up the pathway like the light of day.

2019

Jesus – Light of the World

Two Giants Fell

Two giants fell in Ninety-Four,
That meant a lot to me.
These giants true were Dear Old Dad,
And - the "Good for Nothin' Tree."

Although their limbs were brittle-boned,
Their spirits both were strong.
They still had much to give to us;
Their lives were very long.

Their ages summed to many years;
Dad's next was ninety-three.
And many more than "three score, ten"
Stood - the "Good for Nothin' Tree."

Because the tree was brittle oak
A friend once gave its name.
"That tree is good for nothin';
"You should cut down the same."

Yet there she stood to give us shade
For many years to come.
We all were glad she stood so tall,
Enjoyed by old and young.

Each giant faced so many storms,
And weathered each one well.
But then came storms that blew so hard
That both the giants fell.

Although they're gone, their memories last,
Their strengths will long endure.
We'll not forget their gifts to us.
Their roots in us are sure.

1985

Gentle Jesus

Gentle Jesus, meek and mild,
Look upon this wayward child.
Gentle Jesus, Love thou art,
Come and live within my heart.
Gentle Jesus, strong and sure,
Wash my heart and make me pure.
Gentle Jesus, Once a child,
Make me, like you, meek and mild.

Gentle Jesus, Little Lamb,
Yet thou art the great I Am.
Gentle Jesus, Holy Son,
Thou art God, the only one.
Gentle Jesus, Son of Man,
Hold me in Thy precious hand.
Gentle Jesus, sweet and kind,
I am always on your mind.

Gentle Jesus, free of sin,
His mother, Mary, delivered him,
In a manger, filled with hay,
For the Inn was full that day,
Came to die for sinners, lost,
Gave his life, at what a cost,
Raised to life the third day,
Gentle Jesus paid the way.

Gentle Jesus, Faithful, True,
Help me Lord to be like you.
My example may you be,
Help me keep my eyes on thee.
Gentle Jesus, Prince of Peace,
Cover me with rest and ease.
Then Dear Jesus, lead the way
To your house to live someday.

2018

That's What Jesus Told Me

A little boy lay dying, but no one knew it yet.
His insides were a-wrenching, but soon some help he'd get.
Then a few months later he told His Dad one day,
"Jesus loves the children; that's what I heard Him say."

"Jesus has this round thing that sits upon His head.
"It shines with many colors, like green and blue and red.
"Jesus has some markers. They're on His feet and hands.
"He got them when He came down to die for sinful man."

"That's what Jesus told me. He loves the children, Dad.
"That's why there are many who live with His own Dad.
"We must tell the children who are still here, below.
"That Jesus loves them, dearly. He wants them all to know."

"I got to meet your Pop, Dad and my other sister, too.
"She doesn't have a name yet. It's to come from Mom and you.
"I also saw some animals like horses, dogs and cats.
"Jesus also held me; He sat me in His lap."

"Jesus taught me lessons. He gave me homework, too.
"We have to tell the children. That's us, Dad, me and you.
"Daddy, will you listen, there's more I have to say.
"Jesus loves the children; that's what He said that day."

"That's what Jesus told me. He loves the children, Dad.
"That's why there's so many who live with His own Dad.
"We must tell the children who are still here, below.
"Jesus loves them and He wants the world to know."

Written about the boy in "Heaven is For Real"
2011

My Favorite Season

My favorite season is the spring:
...When life anew is peeking out,
...And colors soft and fresh are clean,
...New hope returns without a doubt,
...And longer nights all flee the scene.

My favorite season is summer:
...Days are bright with azure skies and sun.
...Gardens burst with food and blooms.
...Life fills days with outdoor work and fun,
...And special days for brides and grooms.

My favorite season is the fall.
...As rains refresh the waiting soil,
...Colors dab and paint the trees.
...Harvest brings rewards of toil,
...And thankful pilgrims on their knees.

My favorite season is winter.
...The peace and rest of snowfall's white,
...Renews alike the soul and ground.
...The earth's asleep 'neath blankets, light,
...With sleeping creatures all around.

For the Infant of the Nativity,
Is the Master of Creativity.
Thus every season is the best.
I cannot pick one from the rest.

2009

America - My Crayon Box

My box of crayons tells me so much.
Some are my favorites; some I don't touch.
Some here are broken, others are dull.
Some are named strangely, but that is not all.

Some are real sharp, some nearly gone.
Some are quite pretty, some rather wan.
Yet no two's alike, not even in hue.
And, when one is missing it gives you a clue.

The set's incomplete. Yet, in this box
They all lean together like sheaves set in shocks.
So, just like my country, there's red, white and blue,
But my box has more colors. Of this, it is true.

And though we're all different, together we stand,
In this box of crayons and throughout the land.
We all need each other. This creed I repeat.
It takes the whole box to make it complete.

2011

The Civil War Soldier

He clogs through the mud keeping in line,
Carrying his gun, stepping in time,
Singing a rhyme, or humming a tune,
From daylight to dark and midnight to noon.

He has cuts on his feet and tears in his clothes.
His shoes are worn out and showing his toes.
His stomach is empty, canteen nearly dry.
His thoughts wander home, but dares not to cry.

"When will this be over, this nightmare 'tween men?
I must do my duty, but I wish it would end.
State against state and neighbors at war.
I hardly can stand this, can take it no more."

Yet the young soldier keeps marching on.
Some battles are lost and some battles won.
The snow keeps on falling and freezing his feet.
Or, the sun's bearing down in scorching heat.

He's lost some of his buddies from sickness or strife.
He witnessed today, more than in the rest of his life,
The horror of dying and violence at hand
Brought on by his brother and wielded by man.

His wounds are still hurting, he wished he were dead,
When news of surrender is brought to his bed.
He's weakened and broken but not lost his life.
Just one walk is left and he'll be with his wife.

Now there is hope and reason to live.
The fighting is over, God's praise he did give.
He's witnessed how hatred nurtured the strife,
This "brother's quarrel" has changed him for life.

The battles have ended and treaties are signed,
As peace settles down with hope for mankind.
For a house that's divided surely can't stand.
Each must work together to help understand.

2013
In Memory of my great-grandfather, Henry Wells Spear, who fought
in the Civil War, then walked home to his wife, (from Tennessee to
New York), his health broken for the rest of his life.

Everyone Who Comes Your Way

Everyone who comes your way
Leaves footprints on your soul.
Some will always come to stay,
And others come and go.

Just as the butterfly that flits its wings
Affects the forests' trees -
So, my friends though near or far
Are always blessing me.

2011

The Eagle's Tear

She climbed the currents and soared the skies,
Kept watch o'er nests and her allies,
To help protect those in her world
As she flew forth with wings unfurled.
She cared for all though poor or king
That fell beneath her shadowing wing.
Yet evil lurked throughout the land
And deep inside the heart of man.

They planned their day to maim and kill.
Their goal the eagle's heart to still.
They did not know her strength and skill
Or those who'd rally from her trill,
As she rose up that fateful morn,
The scene she saw filled her with scorn.
She swooped and cawed her mad alarm,
But could not stop that dreadful harm.

Some chicks were hurt and more were dead.
The smoke and fire raged overhead.
What have they done and why choose here,
This land that stands for freedoms dear?
Her heart was pained with what she saw.
Her voice rose up with anguished caw.
Her nest was clawed and torn apart.
Her breast was pierced with guided dart.

The life she knew came crashing down.
Debris rained forth with deafening sound.
The call rang out throughout the world
As to the earth more lives were hurled.
Then from her eyes a tear fell down
Upon her breast of feathered brown,
Her heart was crushed and filled with pain
As smoke rose up from isle and plain,

This monstrous deed made friends from foes
As word rang out about her woes.
They stood with others one and all.
They cursed this deed, which came to maul.
They gave her strength, and came to hail,
"You must not falter; must not fail.
We cannot let them think they've won.
We'll help rebuild, you must go on."

Thus many came from near and far,
They worked beneath both sun and star.
Their hands, their hearts, their all was given,
With strength that came from God in heaven.
So she rose up, her strength renewed,
Shook off the dust to build anew.
She's stronger now and wiser too,
For truth is freedom's best review.

They missed her spirit on that day.
They tried but could not take away
The heart and soul of freedom's flame,
Though still they chant their hate and blame.
Her wounds and scars run deep within
But with God's help she'll heal again.
And through her friends by whom she's loved,
She gains her strength to rise above.

The day, when some had hoped she died,
We'll not forget the eagle cried.
But though she's sad of this be sure,
She will rise up, she will endure.
And though she mourns her loss that day
In depths so deep she did not stay,
But scaled new heights of freedom's skies.
Of this, be sure, the eagle flies!

2001

Native American

I'm a native American,
Born in the land of the free.
I'm a native American,
And proud of my ancestry.

I'm a native American,
For here is where I was born.
I'm a native American,
But not from Indian lore.

Those who were here before
Europeans discovered the land,
Also came from somewhere else,
Moving here from sand to sand.

They're no more native than you or I
If this is where you were born.
No disrespect is proffered here
Or to cause you to be forlorned.

But PC isn't always right,
No matter what they say.
Native American all are we,
If we were born that way.

Let's honor those who came before
As they are part of history,
American Indian is rightly named
For that's what they were thought to be.

We only know what we know
Though often only in part.
Mistakes are made with good intent
But comes from in the heart.

I'm a native American
But those who came 'fore me,
Are our American Indians,
And part of US history.

2019

Peace on Earth

While walking down the neighborhood street,
New fallen snow crunched under my feet.
While freezing night air hit my face when I breathed,
I saw the front doors all decked out with wreaths.
They stood ready to welcome the guests day or night.
The homes through their windows were glowing and bright.

Trees were adorned with ornaments and a bow,
While children heard stories of long, long ago.
A baby was born on a late Jewish night,
While shepherds were blessed by angels of light.
The cattle were lowing and keeping Christ warm,
For God left His glories, and a baby was born.

Rounding the corner on my cold winter stroll,
I thought of remembrances of gone days of old.
I heard the bells ringing from the Church, down the street
As the mat at the door cleaned my cold stomping feet.
I walked in the house and there by the hearth
Christmas music was playing - 'tis "Peace on Earth"!

2013

My Fountain Pen

My fountain pen runs dry
Just when I need it most.
What value does it have
If ink becomes a ghost?

Dear Lord, am I just like my pen
When in Your hand I'm void?
What good am I to You
If inside I'm destroyed?

My child, you do not understand
The value of your "pen."
Let me fill your heart with love
And it will flow again.

An empty vessel you will be
If love's not in your heart.
Then let me hold you in my hand
And let my love impart.

To all mankind on earth
When in my hand you rest,
When I control the use of you,
My children will be blessed.

It's My Son that gives you worth
When your heart you let Him fill.
Things of earth don't satisfy,
But Jesus always will.

2018

One Night, One Room, One Book.

Who loves me?
I thought I knew.
One night rejected,
I hurt all through.

Who loves me?
There's none I thought.
This room's my tomb.
My mind was wrought.

Who loves me?
Soon I would know.
One book fell open,
God's love to show.

Who loves me?
Wiping my eyes,
I looked to the skies,
Accepting God's prize.

Who loves me?
Well, now I know.
'Tis God who loves me.
He died to show.

Who loves me?
Forgiving my sin,
Tis God, Who now
Is living within.

2019
(Testimony of a Gideon)

Pictures of Water

Summer

Puddles. Pools.
Foam. Fun. Spray. Sun.
Tributaries. Sanctuaries.
Waves. Swells. Tides. Wells.
Drips. Drizzles. Drops. Frizzles.
Angry. Gentle. Blinding. Mental.
Flooding. Fury. Torrents. Hurry.
Moisture. Misty. Moody. Mystery.
Cleansing Shower. Energy. Power.
Rolling. Crashing. Pounding. Smashing.
Drowning. Dragging. Dripping. Nagging.
Cascades. Ocean Sprays. Everglades. Dreamy Days.
Embryonic Universe. Unexpected Lightening Burst.

Winter

Peaks. Poles.
Peace. Place. Slow Pace.
Sleet. Slush. Snow. Mush.
Conversation. Transportation.
Crystals. Falling. Quiet. Calling.
Freezing. Chilling. Bone-drilling.
Avalanches. Landscape Blanches.
Crushing. Crafty. Blanket. Drafty.
Glaciers Thawing. Gouging. Clawing.
Farm Pond Skating. Snowman Making.
Ice Blocks. Icebergs. Snow Peaks. Snow Birds.
Snowflakes. Snowfalls. Snowdrifts. Snowballs.

Pictures of Water, continued:

Always

Renewing. Life-giving. Refreshing the Living.
Limpid and languishing. Shallow and Still.
Quietly Laughing. Blubbering. Gaffing.
Boisterously Bawling. Lazily Crawling.
Deep and Moving. Roving at Will.
Death. Strife. Peace. Life.

2011

Motherhood

Dreams, desires, plans and aspirations
Fill our hearts with expectations.

Feedings, fevers, proms and tuitions
Fill our minds with realizations.

Motherhood doesn't turn out the way we hope.
We have joys and tears, then days become years.

But when all is said and all is done,
We're proud of what our children have become.

2011

Corley's Hill

Delivered to Heaven

Just like a babe, delivered in pain,
Passed through the waters and given a name,
Welcomed by family, in Jesus' name.
My journey to heav'n is almost the same.

Death pains are only the labors of birth,
E'en passing through waters when leaving this earth.
My Father will greet me and welcome me there.
He'll hug me and hold me with warm tender care.

I'll put Jesus' face to that wonderful voice.
I'll breath in new air; I'll cry and rejoice.
New garments of white, are waiting, spot free.
He'll show me my home prepared there for me.

I'll drink from the fountain refreshing and clear.
Surrounded by family that I hold so dear.
The saints will rejoice when to heav'n I'm borne.
By angels I'm carried on that wonderful morn.

Loosed from earth's bonds, unfettered at last,
Eyes looking forward, forgetting the past.
What a wonderful day when Jesus I'll see
When to heaven I'm 'birthed;' delivered, and free.

The dark of earth's "womb" aside will be cast.
The "Light of the World" I'll bask in, at last.
For finally I've reached my heavenly home,
Forever to be and no more to roam.

2006

The 23 Psalm of a Pastor

My Pastor is my under-shepherd. Through him, God
shows and provides me what I need.

He shows me where to find green pastures and quiet waters
– spiritual food, rest and refreshment.

His messages from the Lord restore my soul, leading me in
paths of righteousness, for the Lord's name sake.

When I walk through the Valley of Shadows, my Pastor is
there to hold my hand, guide me and pray for me.

When I sin, he teaches me that God loves me, and forgives
me if I confess. If I follow the Lord, I will stay holy and pure.

His prayers and his words from the bible comfort me all the
days of my life.

He teaches me how to defend against my enemies. He tells
me that God is with me and to fear not. He tends to me when
I am wounded and anoints me with his prayers. My heart
runs over with joy.

I am blessed because of the faithfulness of my pastor.
Surely, goodness, mercy and love will fill all the days of my life.
And I will live someday in the house of the Great
Shepherd forever, partly because of God's faithful servant.

Adapted from Psalm 23
2019

The Under - Shepherd

Index:

Printed in the United States
by Baker & Taylor Publisher Services